W9-BNU-937

Hello Incredible Girl!

I'm so glad you want to learn and practice cursive handwriting! Not all schools teach cursive in their curriculum anymore, so this book will walk you through all the beginning steps. Learning cursive is fun, but it also stimulates your brain power! It's a handy skill to have for both kids and adults.

Start off by learning the alphabet, both upper and lower case. On each page you will find a connect-the-dots that will show you the correct way each letter should be written. Writing the letters the correct way will not only help your writing to be easy to read, but you will be able to write faster and more efficiently. There are letters you can practice tracing and plenty of space to write on your own.

Next you will learn how to connect the letters together. Unlike printing, most cursive letters link together and flow. I've chosen combinations of letters that you will likely use often to begin your connecting skills.

Finally, have some fun with it! Practice tracing and writing some words that describe YOU! Fun, fearless, silly YOU! Some words are long, others are short, but as you practice writing your new cursive letters you can be proud of all of your hard work to learn a new skill.

On many pages, you will find a fun picture and a motivational quote. There are also a few coloring pages mixed in the writing pages. Take a minute to let your brain rest and use your creative mind to brighten the pages with color!

At the end of this book, congratulations! You've worked really hard to try something new and you will be ready to move on to a harder book or perhaps write a cursive letter to someone you care about. Remember to let your light shine and always try hard to be the best version of yourself!

Love,
Shannon
Big Dreams Art Supplies

Connect the dots and learn to write the letter

Let's practice!

All your dreams can come true, if you have the courage to pursue them.

Connect the dots and learn to write the letter!

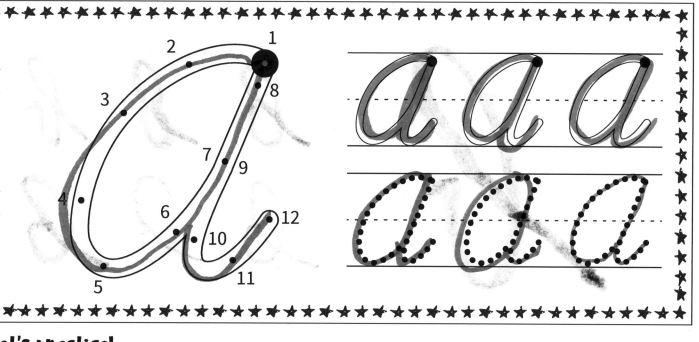

Let's practice!

Say yes to new adventures.

Connect the dots and learn to write the letter

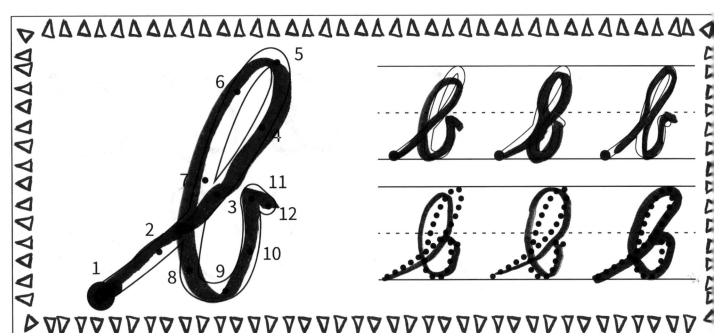

Let's practice!

YES! you can

Be kind whenever possible.

Connect the dots and learn to write the letter!

Let's practice!

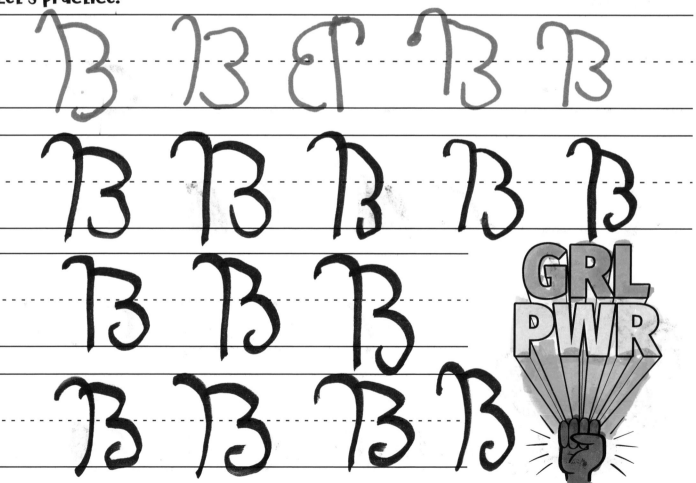

Be brave enough to be yourself!

Connect the dots and learn to write the letter

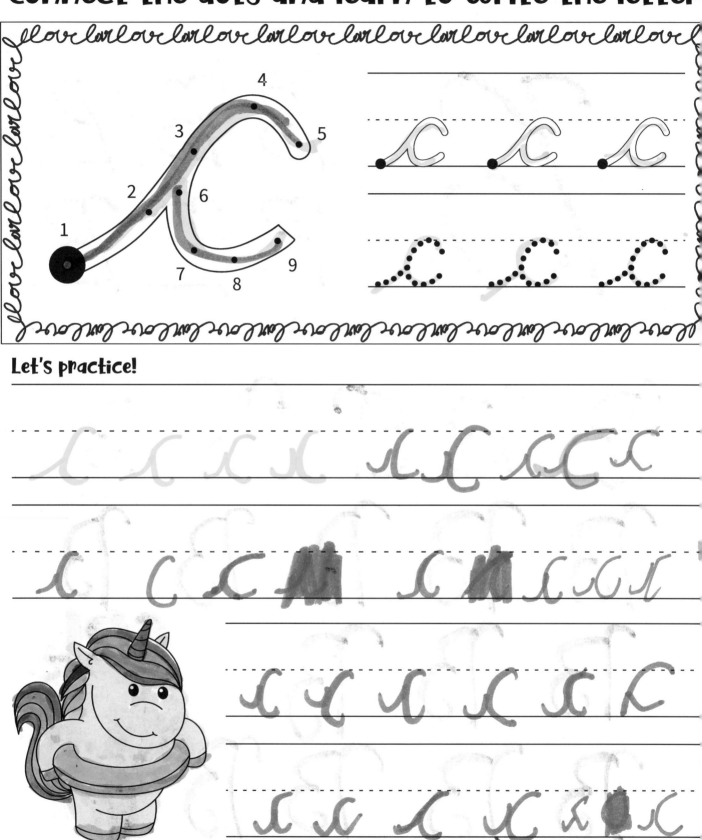

Let's practice!

Courage is being brave, even when you are scared.

Connect the dots and learn to write the letter!

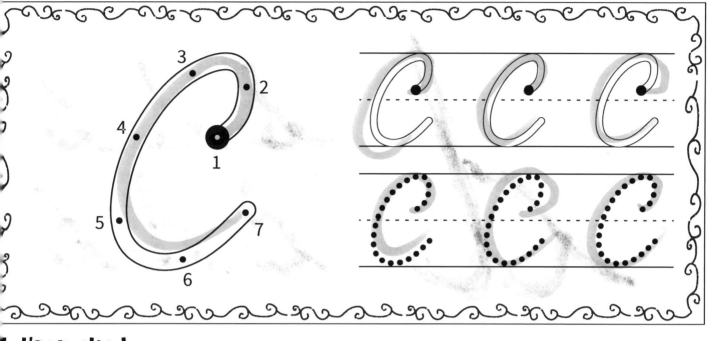

Let's practice!

You can do anything you set your mind to do.

Connect the dots and learn to write the letter

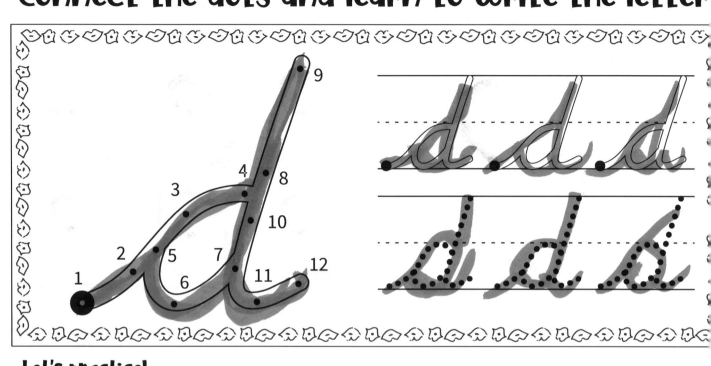

Let's practice!

Dance like nobody is watching.

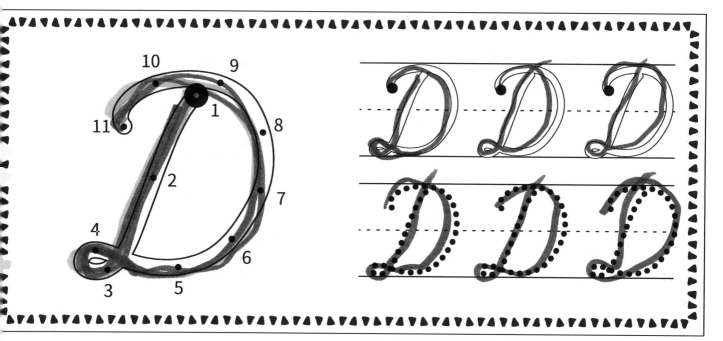

Connect the dots and learn to write the letter!

Let's practice!

Be bold and daring!

Connect the dots and learn to write the letter

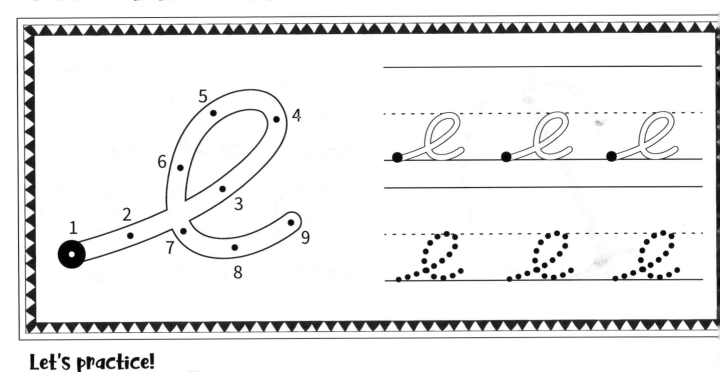

Let's practice!

Everyone is unique.

| $\mathcal{A}$ | $\mathcal{B}$ | $\mathcal{C}$ | $\mathcal{D}$ | $\mathcal{E}$ | $\mathcal{F}$ | $\mathcal{G}$ | $\mathcal{H}$ | $\mathcal{I}$ | $\mathcal{J}$ | $\mathcal{K}$ | $\mathcal{L}$ | $\mathcal{M}$ | $\mathcal{N}$ | $\mathcal{O}$ | $\mathcal{P}$ | $\mathcal{Q}$ | $\mathcal{R}$ | $\mathcal{S}$ | $\mathcal{T}$ | $\mathcal{U}$ | $\mathcal{V}$ | $\mathcal{W}$ | $\mathcal{X}$ | $\mathcal{Y}$ | $\mathcal{Z}$ |
| a | b | c | d | e | f | g | h | i | j | k | l | m | n | o | p | q | r | s | t | u | v | w | x | y | z |

Connect the dots and learn to write the letter!

Let's practice!

Good energy is contagious!

Connect the dots and learn to write the letter

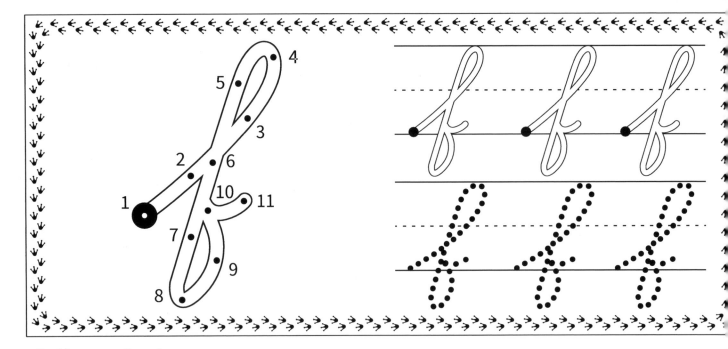

Let's practice!

Focus on your goals to make your dreams come true!

A	B	C	D	E	♡F♡	G	H	I	J	K	L	M	N	O	P	Q	R	S	T	U	V	W	X	Y	Z
a	b	c	d	e	f	g	h	i	j	k	l	m	n	o	p	q	r	s	t	u	v	w	x	y	z

Connect the dots and learn to write the letter!

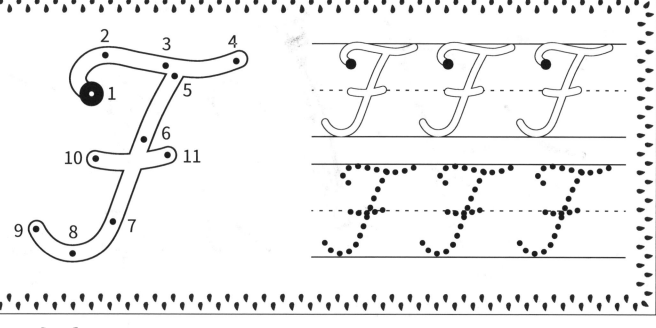

Let's practice!

Be fearless in the pursuit of what sets your soul on fire.

Connect the dots and learn to write the letter

Let's practice!

Grow through what you go through.

Connect the dots and learn to write the letter!

Let's practice!

Keep a fire in your soul and grace in your heart.

Connect the dots and learn to write the letter

Let's practice!

Honesty is the best policy.

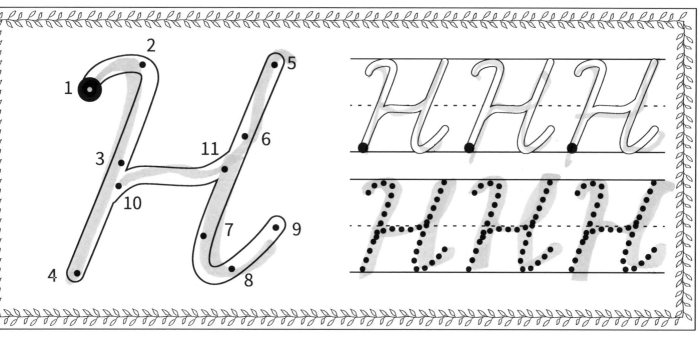

| A | B | C | D | E | F | G | H | I | J | K | L | M | N | O | P | Q | R | S | T | U | V | W | X | Y | Z |
| a | b | c | d | e | f | g | h | i | j | k | l | m | n | o | p | q | r | s | t | u | v | w | x | y | z |

connect the dots and learn to write the letter!

Let's practice!

Choose happiness!

Connect the dots and learn to write the letter

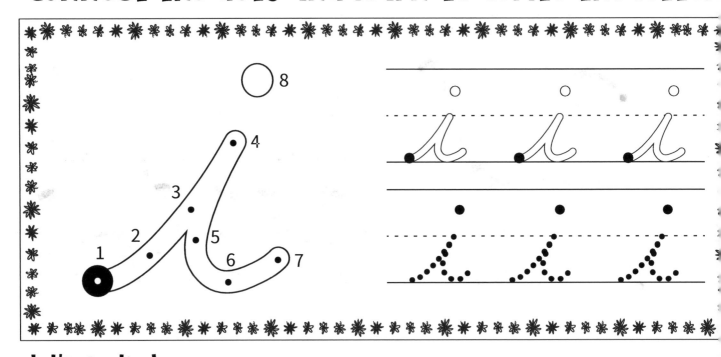

Let's practice!

I am unique. I am special. I am me.

Connect the dots and learn to write the letter!

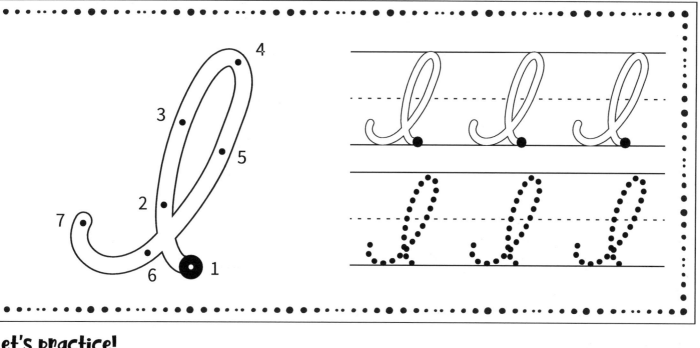

Let's practice!

Your imagination and creativity can change the world.

Connect the dots and learn to write the letter

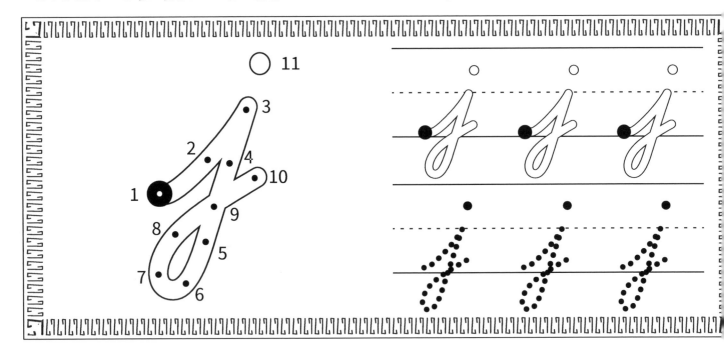

Let's practice!

All your dreams can come true, if you have the courage to pursue them.

A	B	C	D	E	F	G	H	I	J	K	L	M	N	O	P	Q	R	S	T	U	V	W	X	Y	Z
a	b	c	d	e	f	g	h	i	j	k	l	m	n	o	p	q	r	s	t	u	v	w	x	y	z

Connect the dots and learn to write the letter!

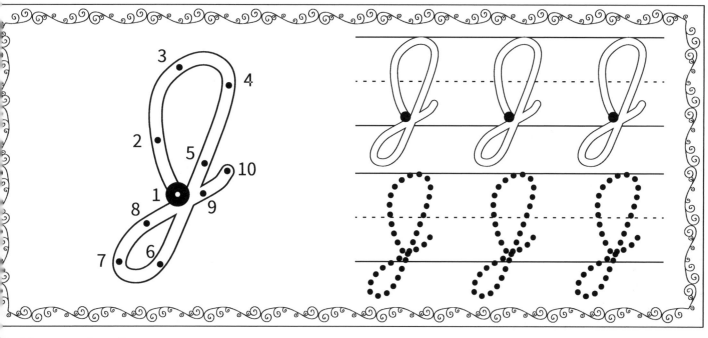

Let's practice!

Have a joyful heart.

Connect the dots and learn to write the letter

Let's practice!

Knowledge is power, so never stop learning.

Connect the dots and learn to write the letter!

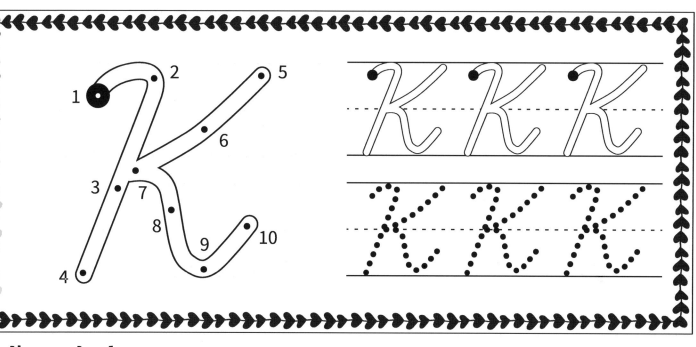

Let's practice!

Sprinkle kindness around like confetti!

A	B	C	D	E	F	G	H	I	J	K	L	M	N	O	P	Q	R	S	T	U	V	W	X	Y	Z
a	b	c	d	e	f	g	h	i	j	k	l	m	n	o	p	q	r	s	t	u	v	w	x	y	z

Connect the dots and learn to write the letter

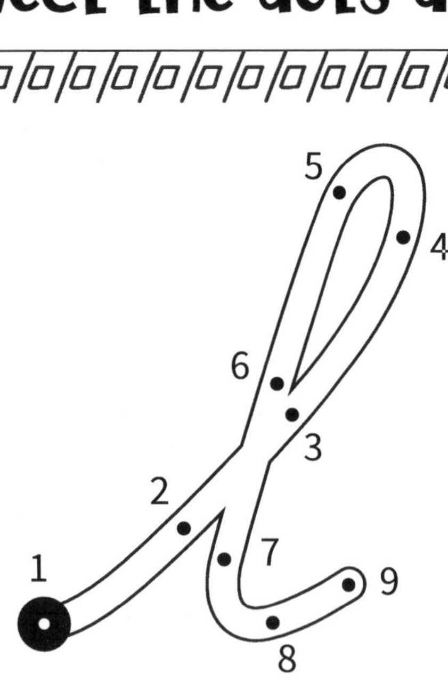

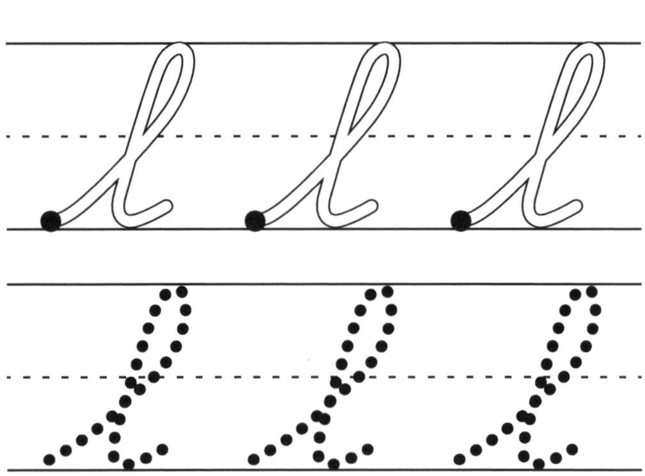

Let's practice!

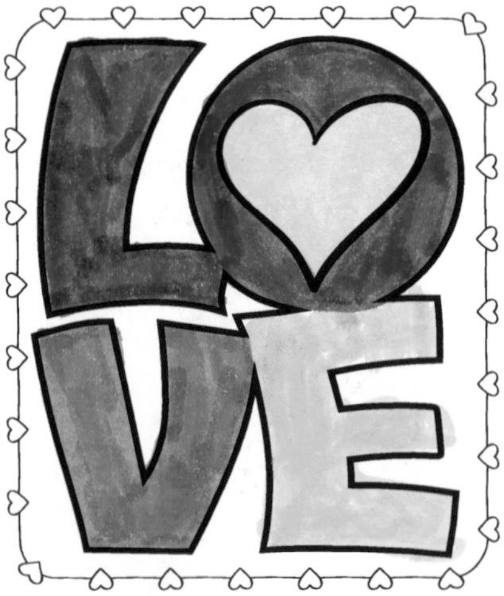

Love without limits.

$\mathcal{A}$	$\mathcal{B}$	$\mathcal{C}$	$\mathcal{D}$	$\mathcal{E}$	$\mathcal{F}$	$\mathcal{G}$	$\mathcal{H}$	$\mathcal{I}$	$\mathcal{J}$	$\mathcal{K}$	$\mathcal{L}$	$\mathcal{M}$	$\mathcal{N}$	$\mathcal{O}$	$\mathcal{P}$	$\mathcal{Q}$	$\mathcal{R}$	$\mathcal{S}$	$\mathcal{T}$	$\mathcal{U}$	$\mathcal{V}$	$\mathcal{W}$	$\mathcal{X}$	$\mathcal{Y}$	$\mathcal{Z}$
a	b	c	d	e	f	g	h	i	j	k	l	m	n	o	p	q	r	s	t	u	v	w	x	y	z

Connect the dots and learn to write the letter!

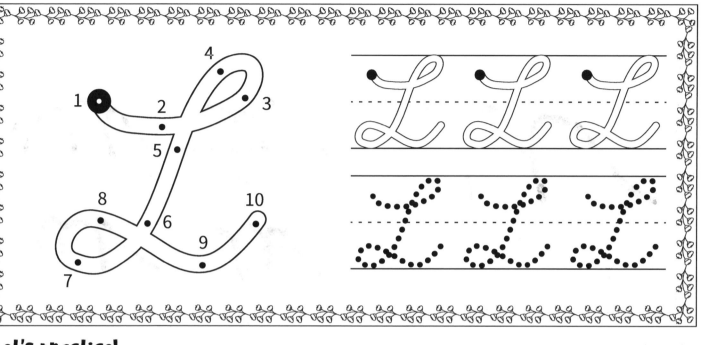

Let's practice!

Laughter is the best medicine!

Connect the dots and learn to write the letter

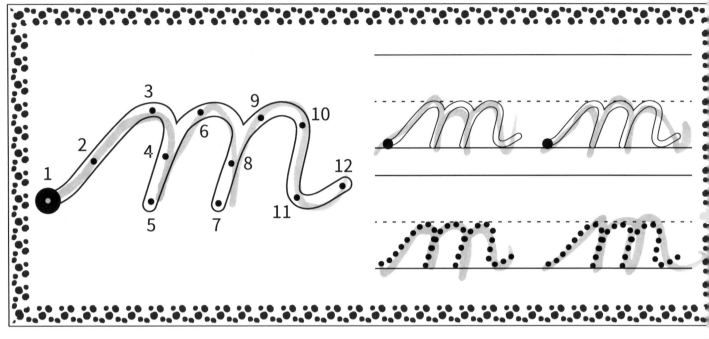

Let's practice!

GIRLS can do ANYTHING

Stay motivated. The harder you work for something, the greater you feel when you achieve

$\mathcal{A}$	$\mathcal{B}$	$\mathcal{C}$	$\mathcal{D}$	$\mathcal{E}$	$\mathcal{F}$	$\mathcal{G}$	$\mathcal{H}$	$\mathcal{I}$	$\mathcal{J}$	$\mathcal{K}$	$\mathcal{L}$	$\mathcal{M}$	$\mathcal{N}$	$\mathcal{O}$	$\mathcal{P}$	$\mathcal{Q}$	$\mathcal{R}$	$\mathcal{S}$	$\mathcal{T}$	$\mathcal{U}$	$\mathcal{V}$	$\mathcal{W}$	$\mathcal{X}$	$\mathcal{Y}$	$\mathcal{Z}$
a	b	c	d	e	f	g	h	i	j	k	l	m	n	o	p	q	r	s	t	u	v	w	x	y	z

Connect the dots and learn to write the letter!

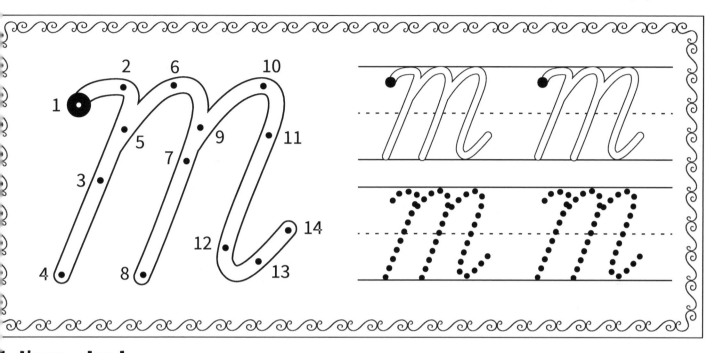

Let's practice!

Make magic wherever you go!

Connect the dots and learn to write the letter

Let's practice!

It is nice to be important, but it's more important to be nice.

$\mathcal{A}$	$\mathcal{B}$	$\mathcal{C}$	$\mathcal{D}$	$\mathcal{E}$	$\mathcal{F}$	$\mathcal{G}$	$\mathcal{H}$	$\mathcal{I}$	$\mathcal{J}$	$\mathcal{K}$	$\mathcal{L}$	$\mathcal{M}$	$\mathcal{N}$	$\mathcal{O}$	$\mathcal{P}$	$\mathcal{Q}$	$\mathcal{R}$	$\mathcal{S}$	$\mathcal{T}$	$\mathcal{U}$	$\mathcal{V}$	$\mathcal{W}$	$\mathcal{X}$	$\mathcal{Y}$	$\mathcal{Z}$
a	b	c	d	e	f	g	h	i	j	k	l	m	n	o	p	q	r	s	t	u	v	w	x	y	z

Connect the dots and learn to write the letter!

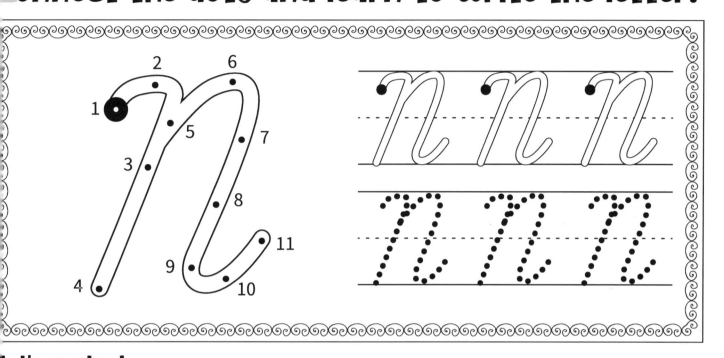

Let's practice!

Undercover Panda

Now is the time to do something amazing!

Connect the dots and learn to write the letter

Let's practice!

Be original. Be yourself.

Connect the dots and learn to write the letter!

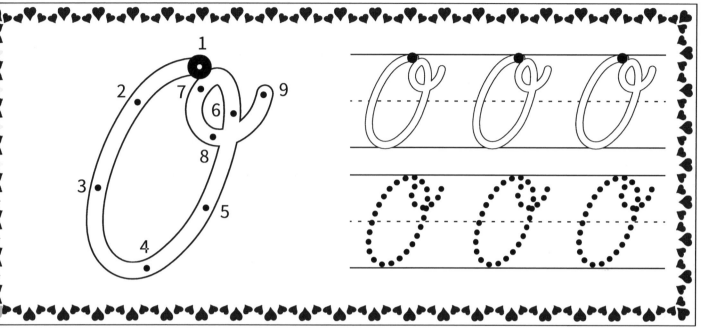

Let's practice!

One person can change the world. Be that person!

Connect the dots and learn to write the letter

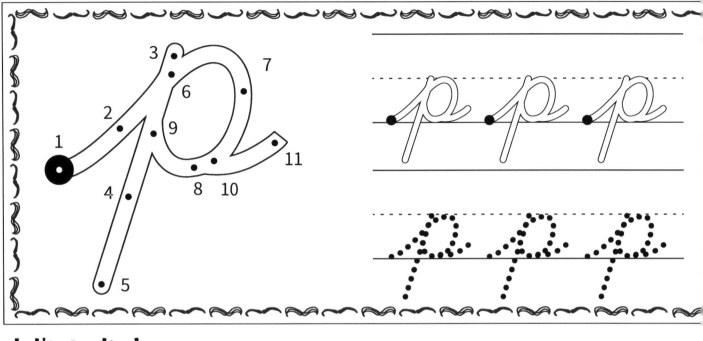

Let's practice!

It doesn't cost one cent to be polite.

Connect the dots and learn to write the letter!

Let's practice!

Play and use your imagination as often as you can.

Connect the dots and learn to write the letter

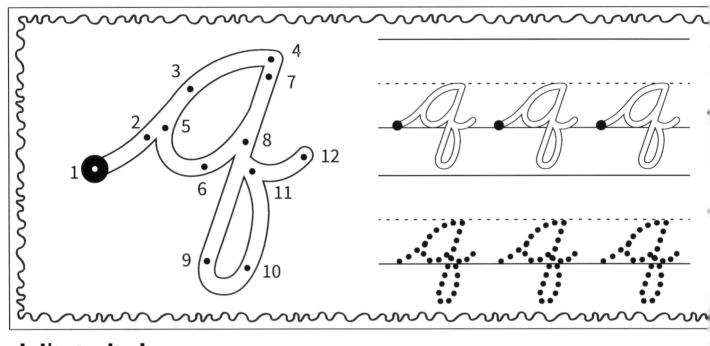

Let's practice!

Admire people who are kind and a little quirky.

Connect the dots and learn to write the letter!

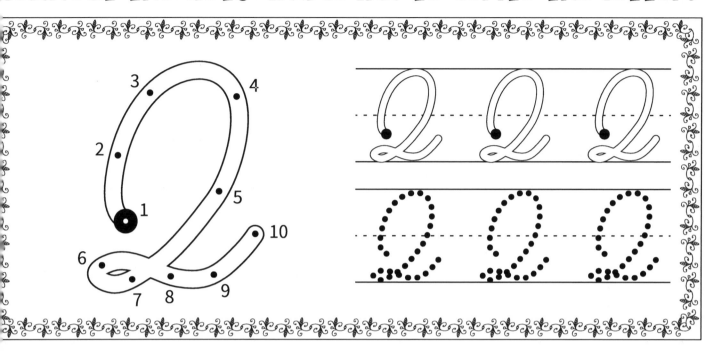

let's practice!

- -

- -

- -

baby
YOU
GOT
THIS

Quick thinking shows confidence and leadership.

| $\mathcal{A}$ | $\mathcal{B}$ | $\mathcal{C}$ | $\mathcal{D}$ | $\mathcal{E}$ | $\mathcal{F}$ | $\mathcal{G}$ | $\mathcal{H}$ | $\mathcal{I}$ | $\mathcal{J}$ | $\mathcal{K}$ | $\mathcal{L}$ | $\mathcal{M}$ | $\mathcal{N}$ | $\mathcal{O}$ | $\mathcal{P}$ | $\mathcal{Q}$ | $\mathcal{R}$ | $\mathcal{S}$ | $\mathcal{T}$ | $\mathcal{U}$ | $\mathcal{V}$ | $\mathcal{W}$ | $\mathcal{X}$ | $\mathcal{Y}$ |
| a | b | c | d | e | f | g | h | i | j | k | l | m | n | o | p | q | r | s | t | u | v | w | x | y |

Connect the dots and learn to write the letter

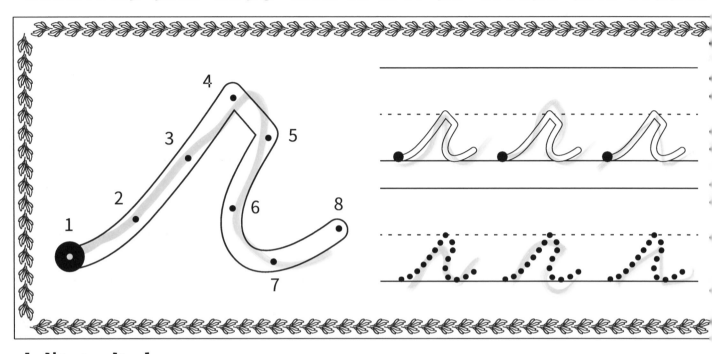

Let's practice!

Take responsible care of the earth. Its the only one we've got!

Connect the dots and learn to write the letter!

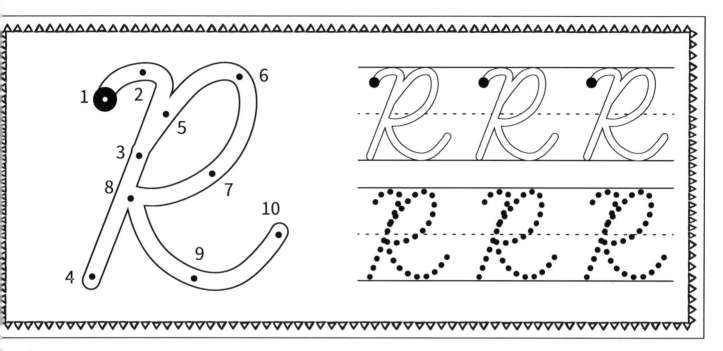

Let's practice!

Respect yourself, and others will respect you.

Connect the dots and learn to write the letter

Let's practice!

Don't ever let anyone dull your sparkle!

Connect the dots and learn to write the letter!

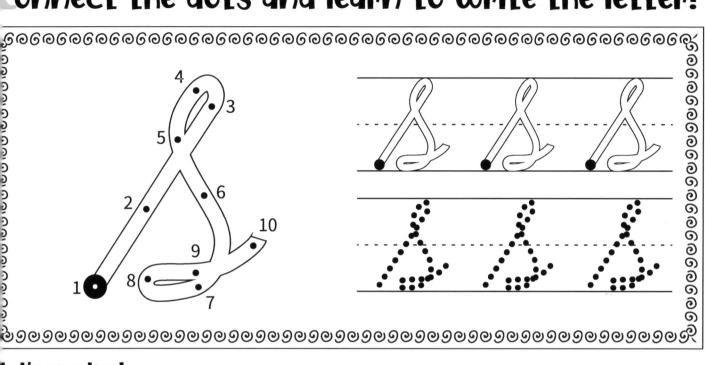

Let's practice!

Girls should never be afraid to be SMART!

Connect the dots and learn to write the letter

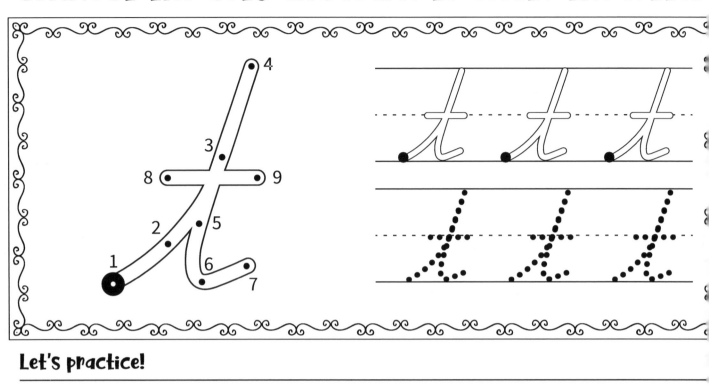

Let's practice!

There's a million fish in the sea, but I'm a mermaid!

Connect the dots and learn to write the letter!

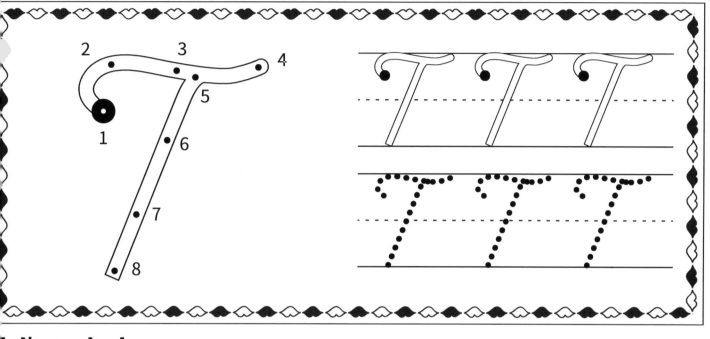

Let's practice!

The best accessory a girl can own is confidence.

Connect the dots and learn to write the letter

Let's practice!

You are magical like a unicorn!

A	B	C	D	E	F	G	H	I	J	K	L	M	N	O	P	Q	R	S	T	U	V	W	X	Y	Z
a	b	c	d	e	f	g	h	i	j	k	l	m	n	o	p	q	r	s	t	u	v	w	x	y	z

onnect the dots and learn to write the letter!

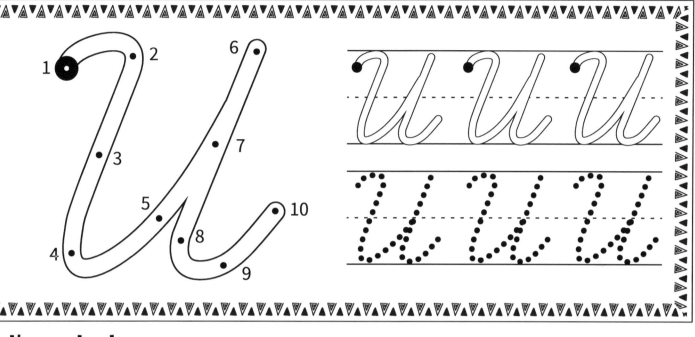

let's practice!

- -

- -

- -

JUST KEEP ROLLING

Unique, unbreakable and unstoppable...they all begin with U!

| $\mathcal{A}$ | $\mathcal{B}$ | $\mathcal{C}$ | $\mathcal{D}$ | $\mathcal{E}$ | $\mathcal{F}$ | $\mathcal{G}$ | $\mathcal{H}$ | $\mathcal{I}$ | $\mathcal{J}$ | $\mathcal{K}$ | $\mathcal{L}$ | $\mathcal{M}$ | $\mathcal{N}$ | $\mathcal{O}$ | $\mathcal{P}$ | $\mathcal{Q}$ | $\mathcal{R}$ | $\mathcal{S}$ | $\mathcal{T}$ | $\mathcal{U}$ | $\mathcal{V}$ | $\mathcal{W}$ | $\mathcal{X}$ | $\mathcal{Y}$ |
| a | b | c | d | e | f | g | h | i | j | k | l | m | n | o | p | q | r | s | t | u | v | w | x | y |

Connect the dots and learn to write the letter

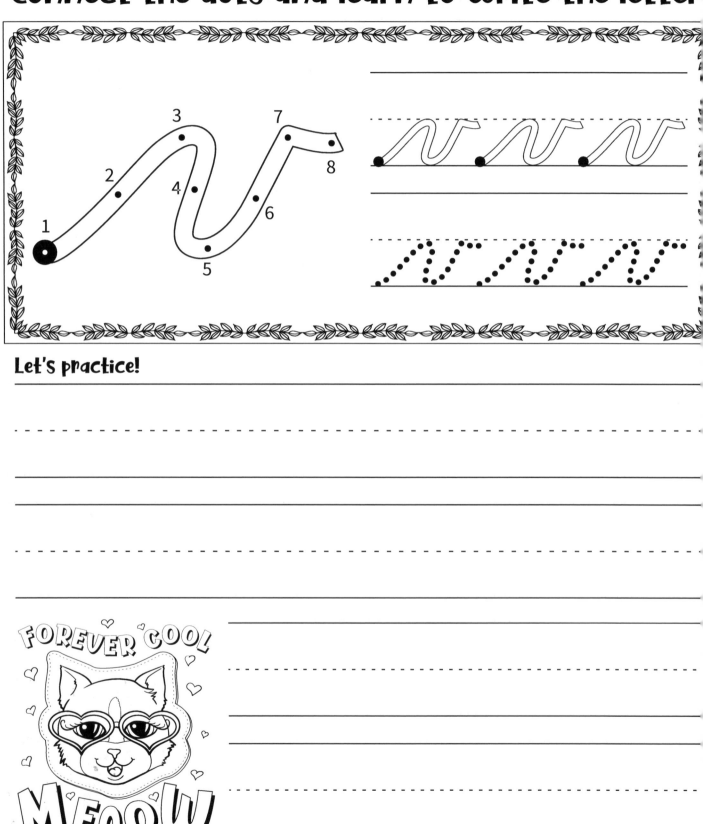

Let's practice!

$\mathcal{A}$	$\mathcal{B}$	$\mathcal{C}$	$\mathcal{D}$	$\mathcal{E}$	$\mathcal{F}$	$\mathcal{G}$	$\mathcal{H}$	$\mathcal{I}$	$\mathcal{J}$	$\mathcal{K}$	$\mathcal{L}$	$\mathcal{M}$	$\mathcal{N}$	$\mathcal{O}$	$\mathcal{P}$	$\mathcal{Q}$	$\mathcal{R}$	$\mathcal{S}$	$\mathcal{T}$	$\mathcal{U}$	$\mathcal{V}$	$\mathcal{W}$	$\mathcal{X}$	$\mathcal{Y}$	$\mathcal{Z}$
a	b	c	d	e	f	g	h	i	j	k	l	m	n	o	p	q	r	s	t	u	v	w	x	y	z

Connect the dots and learn to write the letter!

Let's practice!

Girl POWER

Victory is always possible for the person who fights for it.

Connect the dots and learn to write the letter

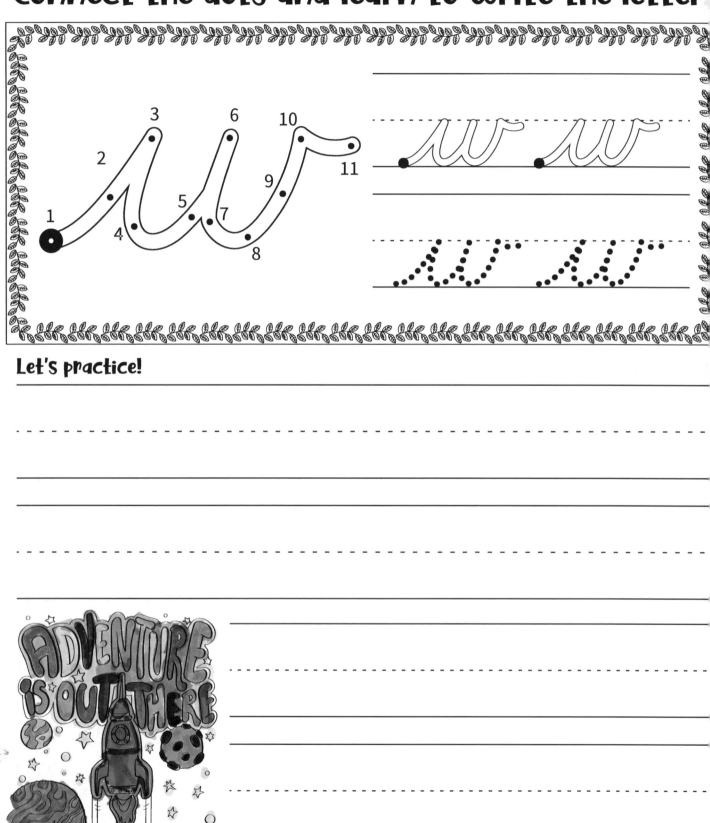

Let's practice!

Those who don't believe in magic will never find it.

$\mathcal{A}$	$\mathcal{B}$	$\mathcal{C}$	$\mathcal{D}$	$\mathcal{E}$	$\mathcal{F}$	$\mathcal{G}$	$\mathcal{H}$	$\mathcal{I}$	$\mathcal{J}$	$\mathcal{K}$	$\mathcal{L}$	$\mathcal{M}$	$\mathcal{N}$	$\mathcal{O}$	$\mathcal{P}$	$\mathcal{Q}$	$\mathcal{R}$	$\mathcal{S}$	$\mathcal{T}$	$\mathcal{U}$	$\mathcal{V}$	$\mathcal{W}$	$\mathcal{X}$	$\mathcal{Y}$	$\mathcal{Z}$
a	b	c	d	e	f	g	h	i	j	k	l	m	n	o	p	q	r	s	t	u	v	w	x	y	z

Connect the dots and learn to write the letter!

Let's practice!

Wish for it, hope for it, dream of it, but by all means DO IT!

$\mathcal{A}$ $\mathcal{B}$ $\mathcal{C}$ $\mathcal{D}$ $\mathcal{E}$ $\mathcal{F}$ $\mathcal{G}$ $\mathcal{H}$ $\mathcal{I}$ $\mathcal{J}$ $\mathcal{K}$ $\mathcal{L}$ $\mathcal{M}$ $\mathcal{N}$ $\mathcal{O}$ $\mathcal{P}$ $\mathcal{Q}$ $\mathcal{R}$ $\mathcal{S}$ $\mathcal{T}$ $\mathcal{U}$ $\mathcal{V}$ $\mathcal{W}$ $\mathcal{X}$ $\mathcal{Y}$ $\mathcal{Z}$

a b c d e f g h i j k l m n o p q r s t u v w x y z

Connect the dots and learn to write the letter.

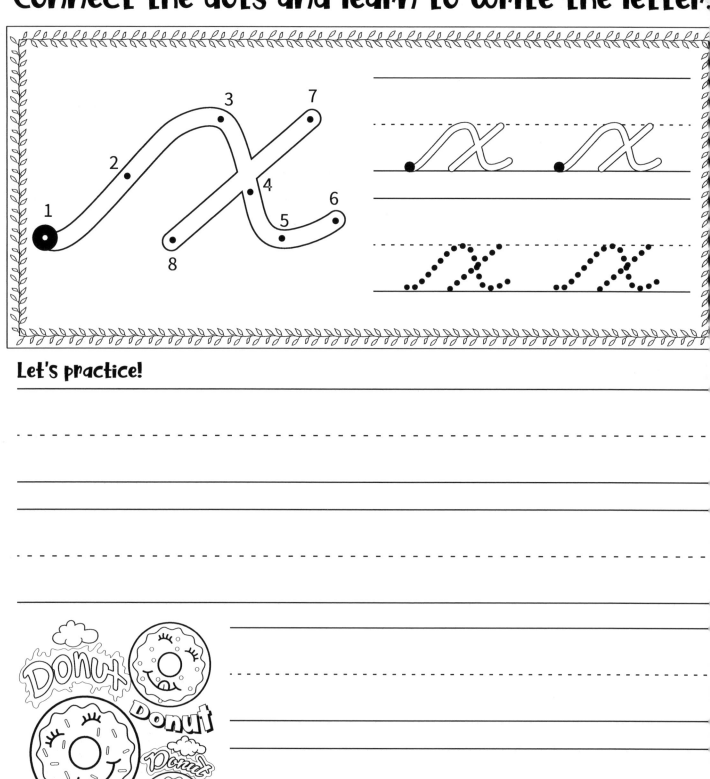

Let's practice!

Stay clever, Little Fox!

Connect the dots and learn to write the letter!

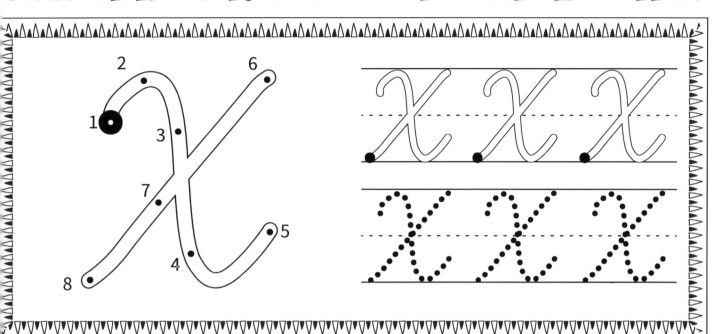

Let's practice!

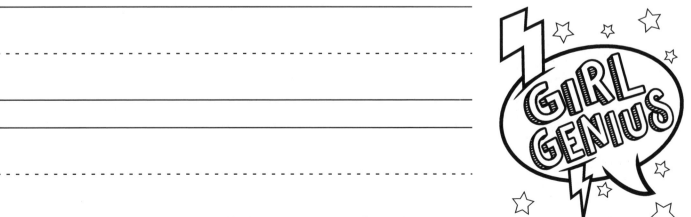

Excellence is doing ordinary things extraordinarily well.

Connect the dots and learn to write the letter.

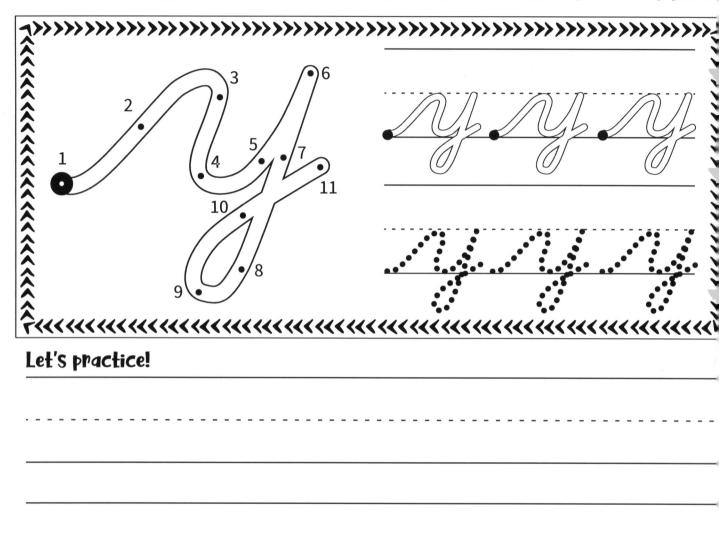

Let's practice!

No one else is you, and that is your super power.

A	B	C	D	E	F	G	H	I	J	K	L	M	N	O	P	Q	R	S	T	U	V	W	X	Y	Z
a	b	c	d	e	f	g	h	i	j	k	l	m	n	o	p	q	r	s	t	u	v	w	x	y	z

Connect the dots and learn to write the letter!

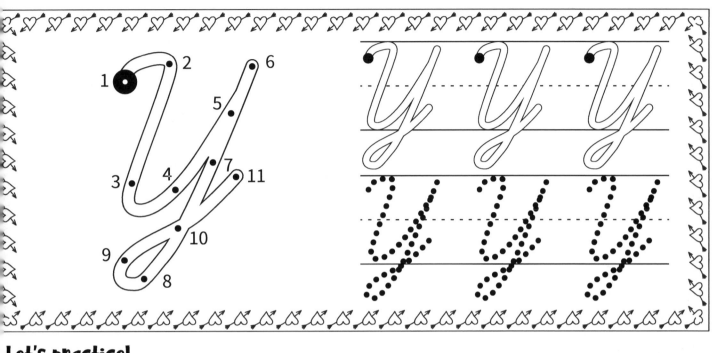

Let's practice!

- -

- -

- -

- -

- -

You can, you should and if you're brave enough to start, you will.

Connect the dots and learn to write the letter.

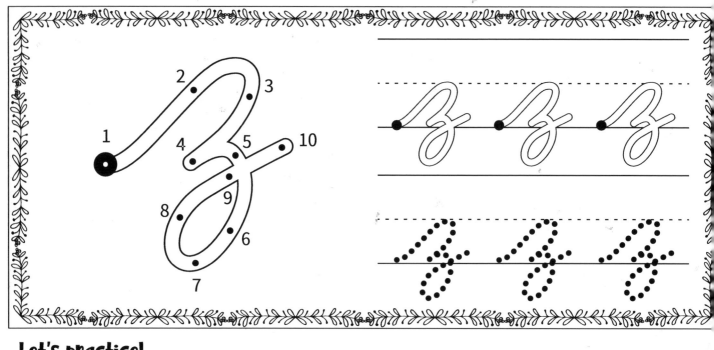

Let's practice!

In a world full of zebras, be a zebricorn!

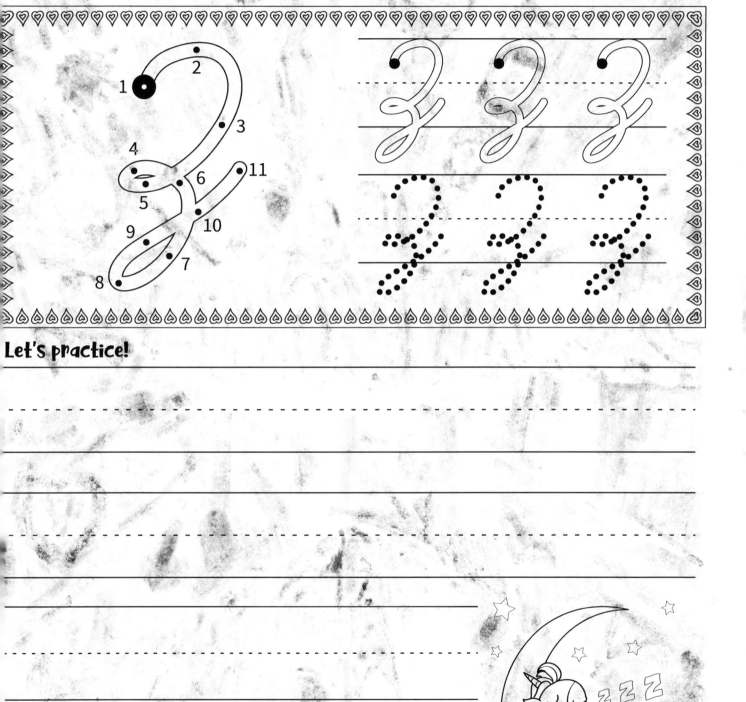

Connect the dots and learn to write the letter!

ABCDEFGHIJKLMNOPQRSTUVWXYZ
abcdefghijklmnopqrstuvwxyz

Let's practice!

Zoom to the moon and let the stars be your light.

Practice Connecting Cursive Letters!

am am

at at

b a ba

b r br

c e ce

c h ch

d e de

d u du

e e ee

Practice Connecting Cursive Letters!

e i ei

f o fo

f r fr

g h gh

g o go

h a ha

h e he

i c ic

i t it

Practice Connecting Cursive Letters!

j i ji

j o jo

k l kl

k o ko

l a la

l l ll

m e me

m o mo

m a ma

Practice Connecting Cursive Letters!

n t nt

o p op

o r or

p r pr

p u pu

q a qa

q u qu

r e re

r k rk

Practice Connecting Cursive Letters!

s k sk

s w sw

t h th

t o to

u n un

u g ug

n e ne

n i ni

w h wh

Practice Connecting Cursive Letters!

wr wr

xo xo

xx xx

ya ya

ye ye

ze ze

zz zz

Practice Connecting Cursive Letters!

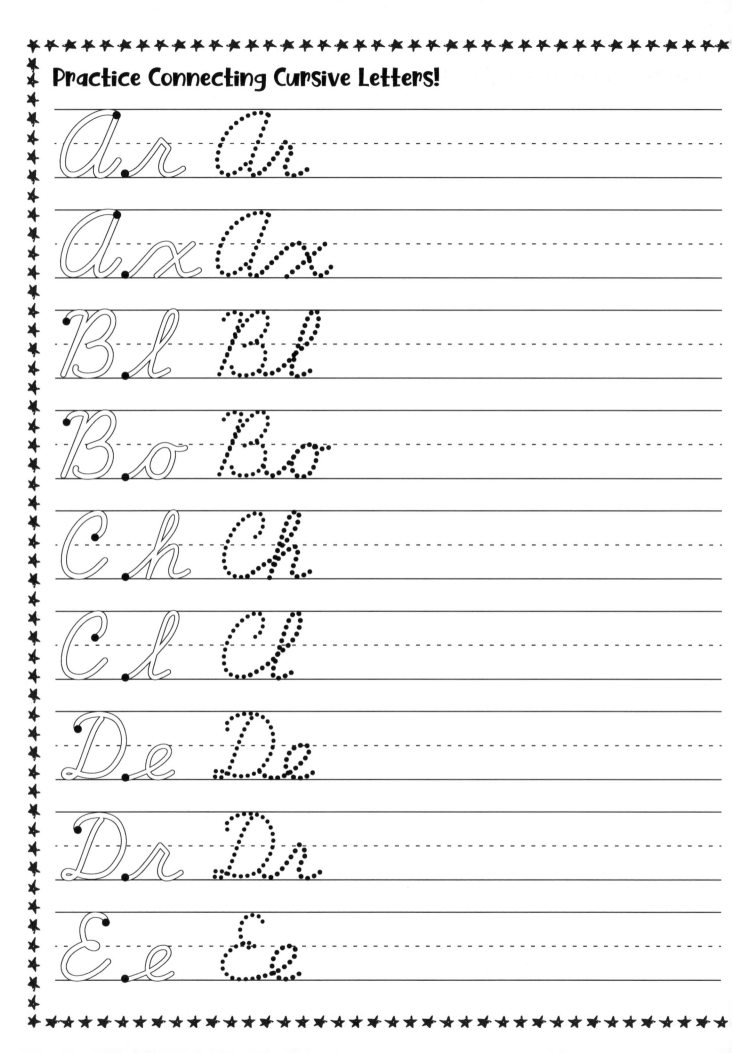

Practice Connecting Cursive Letters!

Eg Eg

Fl Fl

Fo Fo

Ga Ga

Gr Gr

Ha Ha

Hi Hi

Ic Ic

It It

Practice Connecting Cursive Letters!

Ja   Ja

Ju   Ju

Kl   Kl

Ko   Ko

Le   Le

Lu   Lu

Mi   Mi

Mo   Mo

Na   Na

Practice Connecting Cursive Letters!

Ni Ni

Oo Oo

Ot Ot

Pe Pe

Pl Pl

Qu Qu

Qt Qt

Ra Ra

Ru Ru

Practice Connecting Cursive Letters!

Sh Sh

Sp Sp

To To

Tr Tr

Um Um

Up Up

Vi Vi

Vo Vo

Wa Wa

Practice Connecting Cursive Letters!

adventure

Able

bright

Brave

caring

Practice Fun Cursive Words!

Clever

dandy

Daring

energy

Eager

Practice Fun Cursive Words!

friends

funny

giving

Grace

healthy

Practice Fun Cursive Words!

Happy

independent

Imagine

jolly

Joyful

Practice Fun Cursive Words!

know

Kind

love

Laugh

myself

Practice Fun Cursive Words!

Motivated

meat

Nice

outstanding

Original

Practice Fun Cursive Words!

patient

Proud

quirky

Quick

responsible

Practice Fun Cursive Words!

Respect

smart

Strong

tough

Thankful

Practice Fun Cursive Words!

upbeat

Unique

versatile

Vibrant

worthy

Practice Fun Cursive Words!

Wise

Xtra-special

you

Yay

Zany

Practice Fun Cursive Words!

Jealous

Practice Fun Cursive Words!

YOUR REVIEW

What if I told you that just one minute out of your life could bring joy and jubilation to everyone working at a kids art supplies company?
What am I yapping about? I'm talking about leaving this book a review.

I promise you, we take them **VERY seriously**.

Don't believe me?

Each time right after someone just like you leaves this book a review, a little siren goes off right here in our office. And when it does we all pump our fists with pure happiness.

A disco ball pops out of the ceiling, flashing lights come on...it's party time!

Roger, our marketing guy always and I mean always, starts flossing like a crazy person and keeps it up for awhile. He's pretty good at it. (It's a silly dance he does, not cleaning his teeth)

Sarah, our office manager runs outside and gives everyone up and down the street high fives. She's always out of breath when she comes back but it's worth it!

Our editors work up in the loft and when they hear the review siren, they all jump into the swirly slide and ride down into a giant pit of marshmallows where they roll around and make marshmallow angels. (It's a little weird, but tons of fun)

So reviews are a pretty big deal for us.

It means a lot and helps others just like you who also might enjoy this book, find it too.

You're the best!
From all of us goofballs at Big Dreams Art Supplies

|||| ||| |||| |||| |||| ||||

Made in the USA
Middletown, DE
28 November 2020